IT'S GOODNIGHT FROM HIM

Ronnie Barker

THE BEST OF THE TWO RONNIES

illustrated by John Painter · designed by David Cox

HODDER AND STOUGHTON
LONDON · SYDNEY · AUCKLAND · TORONTO

AUTHOR'S ACKNOWLEDGMENT

To Frank Muir:
for helping me to start the Foreword.

To Denis Norden and Marjorie Proops:
for looking so alike.

FOREWORD

"I'd gone to the South of France for six months, to finish my latest book. I'm a very slow reader . . ." Frank Muir, at a formal dinner recently, came out with this beautiful remark; and I laughed so much I dropped blancmange down my wife's dress. (She was pleased about that, because it meant she didn't have to dance with anybody.) It was one of the funniest lines I had heard for a long time - it starts off so pompously and then whips the rug from under itself. And it is this very pomposity that seems to be one of the essential ingredients of comedy.

I find forewords at the beginning of books can very easily become pompous: and as I have no wish for this one to be so, I intend to keep a strict eye on it. I think it very dangerous to conduct a written enquiry into what makes people laugh, because the fact is that anything can make people laugh, if it happens at the right (or wrong) moment. People laugh at funerals. No matter how upset they are, anyone can suddenly be made to giggle at some unexpected occurrence. Anyone except the corpse, that is. Although a corpse in a stage play has been known to get the giggles; and for that reason, if someone laughs when they shouldn't on stage, it is always known as "corpsing" (a fact that few people know — indeed, I wasn't too sure about it myself until I re-read that last sentence). Which mention of the stage leads me, if not neatly, then clumsily in the direction of the following book of sketches, songs, poems, and other trifles which have been performed, from time to time, on "The Two Ronnies". They span six years, and, on looking at the original scripts, I see the early ones are creased and crumpled, while the later ones are fresh, shining and unmarked. Then I look at photographs of Ronnie and me over the same period and find exactly the opposite. "Ah well," as someone once remarked, "that's life, with a capital F."

Ronnie Barker

1976

Contents

HOTEL LOUNGERS

A General and an Admiral sitting in an hotel lounge; a tea-time trio is playing. They sit, in uniform, in two easy chairs; they are very old. A pretty waitress in a short skirt delivers tea to the Admiral. The General ogles her legs. She goes.

R.B. (Admiral): Thank you, Dulcie.

R.C. (General): Nice legs.

R.B.: Yes, very good tone, as well.

R.C.: What?

R.B.: The piano.

R.C.: No, the waitress. Nice legs.

R.B.: A trim craft. Fond of women are you?

R.C.: I used to be.

R.B.: Gone off 'em, have you?

R.C.: Not at all. Just as keen as ever.

R.B.: It's just opportunity, really, isn't it?

R.C.: Yes. Lately I never seem to get the chance to show my prowess.

R.B.: How long is it?

R.C.: What?

R.B.: How long is it? – since you had, since you made, since you were, er . . . since you did, er . . . the . . . er . . . made love. To a woman, I mean.

R.C.: I don't see that's any of your business.

R.B.: No, no. I'm sorry.

R.C.: Since *you* did, I bet a pound.

R.B.: What?

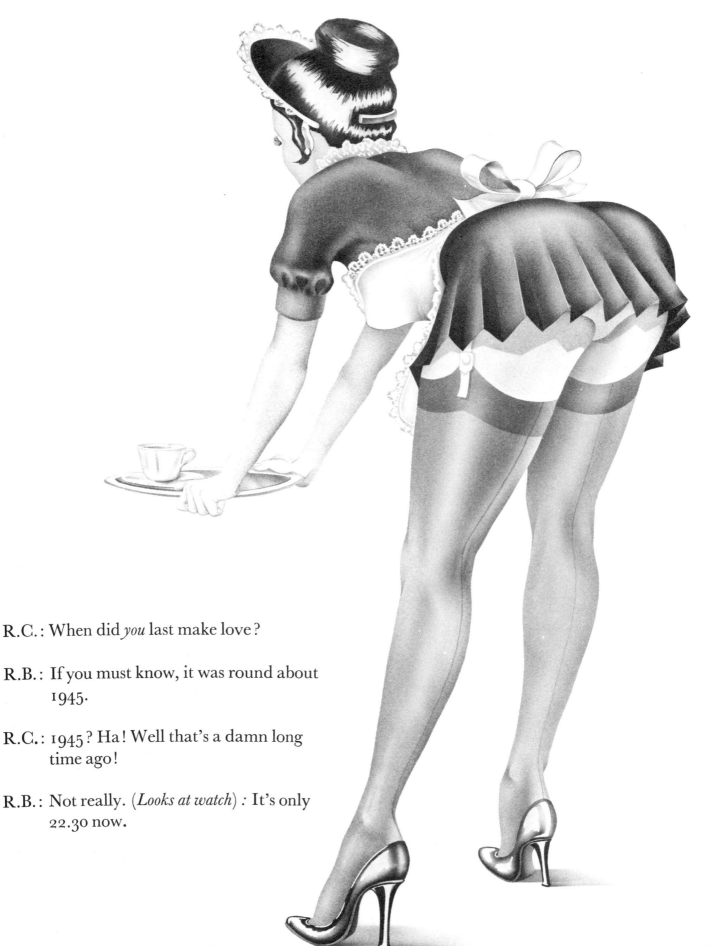

R.C.: When did *you* last make love?

R.B.: If you must know, it was round about 1945.

R.C.: 1945? Ha! Well that's a damn long time ago!

R.B.: Not really. (*Looks at watch*) : It's only 22.30 now.

A Greengrocer's Shop

R.B. is just finishing serving a woman, tipping brussel sprouts into her shopping basket. R.C. enters, and approaches R.B.

R.C.: Two pounds of King Edwards, please.

R.B.: Right guv. (*He weighs them out.*) Lovely, these are.

R.C.: Yes, they look excellent. Could I have them gift-wrapped please.

R.B.: Eh?

R.C.: They're a present for someone.

R.B.: Oh. Oh. Er . . .

R.C.: You know – bit of coloured paper, nice fancy box, something of that sort. Makes all the difference, doesn't it?

R.B.: Oh, it does, guv, yeah. I don't know what I've got . . .

R.C.: Well, leave it for the moment, there's some more things I want. Er – have you got anything suitable for an old aunt?

R.B.: Er – well . . .

R.C.: . . . sits on her own a lot and doesn't do much.

R.B.: How about some prunes?

R.C.: No. I don't think so. Hardly the sort of thing one gives as a present is it? A prune. No – I know. A cabbage. That's always acceptable, a nice big cabbage.

R.B.: Right – how's that one? (*Shows him cabbage.*)

R.C.: Fine, she'll like that. Now then, Mummy.

R.B.: Mummy? Your Mummy?

R.C.: Yes. She's so difficult. She's got everything. Absolutely everything.

R.B.: (*Thinks for a second then –*): I bet she hasn't got any celery.

R.C.: Yes, she has. Plenty.

R.B.: Tomatoes?

R.C.: No, I gave her those last year.

R.B.: Oh.

R.C.: She's still got some left.

R.B.: I've got it. What about a nice avocado. Perhaps a pair?

R.C.: An avocado is a pear.

R.B.: No, I mean two avocado pears, set in straw, side by side. Sort of presentation case.

R.C.: It's not a bad idea.

R.B.: (*Showing him*) : Look at those. They'd do anybody's mother proud, they would.

R.C.: (*Looking at them*) : You haven't got any white ones, have you?

R.B.: White ones? You don't get white ones, not in the avocadoes.

R.C.: Oh, you see, she lives in Cheltenham. I don't know what the neighbours might think if they found out she's got a couple of black avocadoes in the house.

R.B.: They're green – dark green, these.

R.C.: Yes, I suppose they are. All right. I'll take them – it's about time she learned to be a bit more broad-minded, anyway. Now then, Uncle Willy.

R.B.: Ah. What's he like?

R.C.: Well, he's a very heavy smoker.

R.B.: What about a few artichokes. That would be a laugh.

R.C.: (*Laughing*) : Yes, it would, that's marvellous. (*R.B. starts to put some into a bag.*) Just a minute, what's funny about an artichoke?

R.B.: Hearty Choke. Heavy smoker. You see? Arti-choke! (*He coughs and splutters.*) Choke! Hearty . . . how about a marrow?

R.C.: Yes, all right. Now, do you send vegetables by wire?

R.B.: No.

R.C.: No Interveg, or Cauliflora, or anything like that?

R.B.: No.

R.C.: Only I've got these relatives in Australia, and they miss their spring greens at Xmas.

R.B.: Don't they get spring greens in Australia.

R.C.: Only in the summer, you see. That's the way it works out. Well, never mind. Have all these items sent round to this address, would you? (*Gives him a card.*) Nice to get one's Xmas shopping done all in one go, isn't it?

R.B.: Yes, isn't it?

(*R.C. goes, and immediately returns.*)

R.C.: I am silly, bought all those things and I haven't got myself anything for lunch today. How much are the chrysanthemums?

PLAIN SPEAKING

A spokesman desk, as on T.V. R.B. enters in old-fashioned dinner jacket, drunk. A Floor Manager sits him in the chair.

FM: (*Whispering*) *:* We're just about on the air, Sir Harry. Your speech is on autocue.

RB: What? (*Clutches notes in his hand.*) *:* I've got me notes.

FM: No, look, the words on the prompter there, all written up. Just read them out. I'll take those. (*Tries to get notes.*)

A SPOKESMAN FROM
MIN. OF COMMUNICKATIONS

RB: Get off! (*He snatches them away and they fall on the floor. He bends to pick them up. Music starts ; cut to close-up of R.B.'s rear. Superimpose the caption "A SPOKESMAN". R.B. turns, recovers, starts to speak.*)

Good . . . er . . . it is – evening. I am a . . . er . . . spokesman for the Ministry of . . . er . . . what is it – Communications. And we all thought it would be a good idea, if I came along this evening, and told you all, what was, I mean, tried to explain the whole . . . er . . . put you, in it. The hole. The picture. As to what the f- what the folk, up at the Ministry think they're pl- think they're doing — know they're doing, because I am one of *them. One* of them. And I should know what I'm doing, but I don't. Want you to think that we at the . . . er . . . where is it – the Ministry are sitting down on our fat . . . er . . . fat chance we get to sit down at all because we are *constantly* on each others toes, and secretaries, are, I mean she's always buzzing around, making tea and ends meet and giving her utmost I mean most of her ut. Not that I want you to think. That we *have* anything. To hide. The Ministry of, er . . . Communickers, Commu Knickers, cam-knickers, cami-knickers, cami-knickasians is not a – cannot be compared with a, I mean is nothing like, a . . . er . . . Water closet. Er . . . water, gate, Watergate. Nobody's going round bugging each other, thank goodness, because, I mean, these people who do go around, bugging other people are, er, I mean they are absolute b-, er . . . I mean there's only one word to describe them, and that is . . . er . . . they are simply . . . er . . .

rotten bugbears. As the Minister himself said, "We don't want any bugs in this Ministry. I'm the only big bug around here" and he's absolutely, er . . . parched. Er . . . perfectly right. I say, it's absolutely stifling in here – does anybody mind if I open a bottle? Thanks. (*He takes a half bottle whisky flask*

from his pocket, pours whisky into carafe glass. Picks up carafe pours water into glass as well. As he puts down the carafe, the Floor Manager's hand comes and takes the glass away. Not even noticing this R.B. drinks from the whisky flask.) That's better. Now, thirdly, I come to my second point. Inflation. The Prime Minister, of whom it has been said – many times – and indeed, who am *I* . . . I repeat, who am *I* . . . (*He looks inside his jacket to read name.*) Oh, yes. Who am I, a mere Moss Bros, to argue with him? He said, at the last Common Market assembly and here I quote, (*Looks at notes.*) "Trousers to cleaners, liquid paraffin, boots." And what a sorry picture that presents of the country today. We stand figuratively speaking at the crossroads. The men and women of this country having been taken to the cleaners, trouserless, not knowing which way to look – to turn; and some of us are already . . . er . . . on the turn, slipping and sliding our boots filled with liquid paraffin, on the downwards path that leads to the upward spiral of inflation, knowing that we must move, in ever decreasing circles, finally

disappearing up our only chance, is to stand firm, and sleep it off – sweat it out. Back to back, noses to the wall, best foot forward, knees together and legs astride, we must all push in the same direction, see, and I would be the first to join in the fun, bearing in mind . . . er . . . that I include women in this, because women are, in a sense, lumped together. At least, the ones I know are. Finally, in confusion I would like to say unrequir, unrequilier, but I can't. But what I can say is this. Peace, perfect peace – that's what we all want. And we cannot get it alone. We must combine with the rest of Europe; in a spirit of comradeship and conviviallity. And that is why I am meeting the French Minister for Communications directly after this broadcast. In his own words, "We go out and get peace together". Good night.

JOLLY
RHYMES
(LIMITED)
BIRTHDAY CARD MANUFACTURERS

Inside the office of
JOLLY RHYMES (LTD)
sits a man (R.B.)
dictating to Miss Green,
a heavy girl in tight trousers.

R.B.: Lots of lovely things to eat
And lovely games to play,
Greetings to my birthday boy
You're 46 today.

(Knock on door.)

R.B.: Come in, come in.
(Enter R.C.) : Ah! Arthur Jones.
　　　　　Good morning, how are you?
Sit down, sit down, and hurry up
　　　　　I've lots of work to do.

R.C.: I'm sorry to disturb you, George.

R.B.: Think nothing of it, lad!
Cheer up, come, come! don't look so glum
　　　　　I'm sure it's not *that* bad.

R.C.: It's just that I've been thinking, and
　　　　　I've just come in to state,
We shouldn't go on using rhymes
　　　　　On cards – it's out of date.

R.B.: What's that? No rhymes on birthday cards?
　　　　　Come have you lost your mind?
Now please don't waste our time lad, you
　　　　　can see Miss Green's behind.

(So can we – she is bending over a filing cabinet.)

R.C.: You see? You even speak in verse;
It could destroy your health.
This thing has gone from bad to worse –
I'm doing it myselth.

R.B.: I say, now, now, there's no need to
Exaggerate, old chap
I do not *always* speak in rhyme
That's just a load of rubbish.

But birthday cards, without a rhyme!
No, no, out of the question.

R.C.: Oh, well, I thought I'd mention it –
T'was only a suggestion.

R.B.: (*Leading him out*):
And very welcome too, of course!
It's always nice to know,
That folk are thinking on the job.
Bye, Bye! Mind how you go!

(*He shuts door on R.C.*)

Miss Green: Well, strike a light – of all the nerve!
I think that's a disgrace!
I know I'm new round here, but still
I'd put *him* in his place.

Tell him to take a running jump
Obnoxious little worm!

R.B.: Now, you be careful what you say –
He owns the flaming firm.

A church hall stage. Banks of huge Hydrangeas;
and banks of Ladies, some huge, some tiny. They
are all dressed alike. They all hold music books.

R.B. and R.C., as two of the ladies, with corsages
of roses pinned to their bosoms.

The choir starts with "Nymphs and Shepherds", in
time to the music.

R.B.: Cynthia Shepherd has gone away,
     Gone away.

R.C.: Where's she gone?

R.B.: Her mother won't say.
     Saturday she packed and went away.

R.C.: Denis Grove,
     Denis Grove across the way,

He went away, on Saturday.
Now wait, I know what you're going
to say,
'Praps he went on holiday.

R.B.: Yes and Cynthia met him halfway.

R.C.: That's not like Cynthia at all,
     She's not the sort of girl to muck about.

R.B.: You're joking!
     I've often seen her stop and take a
     bloke in.

R.C.: Oh Elsie!
     He'd really have to urge her, 'cos her
     father is a verger
     And her mother is a vegetarian.

R.B.: The daft young cow.

ALL:
Oh dear, what can the matter be?

R.C.:
I went to the hairdressers Saturday,
There we sat like hens in a battery,
While the young man did our hair.

The first one to do me his name it was Michael,
He wanted to give me a ride on his cycle,
And much as I'd like a good cycle with Michael,
I don't trust his cross-bar so there.

The second one *he* was a Welsh boy called Billy,
He wanted to show me the hills of Caerphilly,
I wouldn't trust Billy beyond Piccadilly,
There's no mountain climbing up there.

The Manager thought that he'd just keep his
hand in,
He promised to show me his flat on the landing,
But when we got there it was nothing
outstanding
In fact quite a pokey affair.

Oh dear, I learnt on Saturday,
No good, responding to flattery,
That won't recharge your battery,
I'll do my own bloody hair.

R.C.: Now now now, now now now, now
now now,
It'll turn out right you'll see.

R.B.: Oh, very well
But time will tell.

R.C.: You are just as bad as me,
You are always putting
Two and two together and making
three.

R.B.: Just remember what I say,
Come what may,
She'll be in the family way
One fine day
That's why she's gone away!

(*Polite applause. The ladies cough discreetly and
prepare for the next item on the agenda.*)

(The lady pianist immediately tinkles out the opening bars of the final song, the ever-popular "Pipes of Pan".)

R.C.: Have you heard about young Mandy
At the annual dinner dance?

R.B.: Hurry up and tell me what, what, what.

R.C.: Someone laced the punch with brandy
And she never stood a chance.

R.B.: Drunk she got, silly clot.

R.C.: Lost an earring in a fight.

R.B.: Thats not all she lost that night,
A policeman so they say
Found her knickers a mile away
In Harrow,
On someone's barrow
Wrapped round a marrow
Marked half-a-crown.

ALL: Oh-h-h . . .

R.B.: Hurry, hurry, hurry, I've got to go
and cook a flan,
My husband Keith has lost his teeth
He flushed them down the pan,
In the can –

R.C.: I'll speak to Anne, her husband Dan's
The sanitary man
You never know where they may
turn up

BOTH: In –

ALL: The merry, merry pipes of Pan!

(The voices swell up in sweet harmony, to the final top notes.)

Magic Ring

A little man stands in a shabby room.
He is holding a gaudy piece of jewellery
in his hand.
He begins to chant.

MAN:
Magic Ring, O Magic Ring,
grant me, grant me just one thing.
Make my wife twice as pretty,
twice as smart, twice as intelligent,
and twice as sexy as she is now!

(Enter ugly, untidy, stupid, frigid woman.)

WOMAN:
Oi. Yer dinner's ready, when yer want it.

MAN:
My God! It works!

(He rushes to her and clasps her to him.)

A Reply To The Previous Toast

R.B.: My friends – or may I call you ladies and gentlemen. I have been asked to make a speech; but before I do, I'd like to say a few words. And before I do *that*, I tell I *must* feel you, that I've had a few. Drinks, that is, not words. Mind you, quite a few words have passed my lips too, in my time. And what a marvellous invention it is, isn't it? The spoken word. The spoken word! Through this method, I can instantly transmit my thoughts to you all, wherever you may be. And you may be anywhere. In fact, at this moment, er . . . most of you are. And for those of you who are not, keep trying.

Now it's essential that we know what's going on, and indeed, what isn't going on that should be. We must communicate with each other, and also with anyone else we happen to meet, because everyone – and by everyone I mean everybody can, and in fact does, or if they don't at present they very soon will,

because to be honest, everyone has to, eventually, for, as we all know, and those who've had the experience will bear me out. And the sooner the better. What I mean to say is, if we all stand up and say what we mean, and, at the same time, are prepared to sit down and listen to what everyone else is saying, and then turn round and give an honest reply, we shall be stepping forward, all together, and standing up, and turning round, and sitting down, all over the world, as one man. And what a sight that would be! Especially if the women joined in. Because, obviously, women are, in a sense, lumped together.

In other words, we must try to regard the nation as a whole. And those who think it *is* one, should get out and make room for the others, because, I mean, statistics prove that if that population goes on – exploding – that is to say if people keep on having – I mean if men and women don't stop – if young married couples continue to – I mean and who can blame them. Good luck to them. Man cannot live by bread alone, but nevertheless, it's his job to get out and *win* it, and it's the woman's place to stay at home and butter it for him. Nowadays, it is becoming the thing for women to follow a career – and this could lead to trouble. Mind you, I'm not denying that some women have a perfect right. But, on the other hand, they've got an equally good left, and why – where do women get these ideas, about wanting to wear the trousers? In my opinion they should drop them completely, and assume their rightful position – bent over the sink. I mean when a man gets back after a hard sleep at the office, he doesn't want to find his wife out – er – out trying to earn enough to keep body and legs together, because statistics prove that eighteen per cent of the working men in this country . . . er . . . are women. And if that isn't proof of the pudding, if proof were needed, then I don't know, who has.

To sum up:

You may drink to the girl with the face
that's divine;
To the girl with the figure what's wavy –
You may drink to the girl from blue-
blooded stock;
You may drink below stairs, with the
slavey.
You may drink to the girl who is one of
the boys
Who goes out with the army and navy;
But here's to the girl who is both rich
and old –
To the girl with one foot in the gravy.

Ladies and gentlemen – absent friends!

(*He drinks.*)

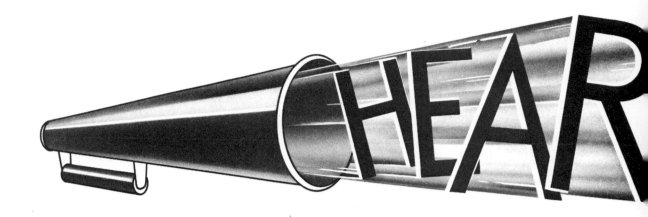

R.B. sits at desk. A large sign on the wall –
"HEARING-AID CENTRE". Enter R.C.
He approaches the desk.

R.C.: Is this the hearing-aid centre?

R.B.: Pardon?

R.C.: Is this the hearing-aid centre?

R.B.: Yes, that's right, yes.

R.C.: Ah. I've come to be fitted for a hearing-aid.

R.B.: Pardon?

R.C.: I say I've come for a hearing-aid.

R.B.: Oh, yes. Do sit down. I'll just take a few details. Name?

R.C.: Pardon?

R.B.: Name?

R.C.: Crampton.

R.B.: Pardon?

R.C.: Crampton.

R.B.: Oh, Crampton.

R.C.: Pardon?

R.B.: I said Crampton.

R.C.: Crampton, yes.

R.B.: Right, Mr. Crampton. Now I take it you are having difficulty with your hearing.

R.C.: Pardon?

R.B.: I say, I take it you're having difficulty with your hearing.

R.C.: That's correct.

R.B.: Pardon?

R.C.: I say that's correct.

R.B.: Which ear?

R.C.: Pardon?

R.B.: Which ear?

R.C.: The right.

R.B.: Pardon?

R.C.: The right ear.

R.B.: Ah. Could you cover it up with your hand please. (*He does so*):
Now, can you hear me?

R.C.: Pardon?

R.B.: Can you hear what I'm saying?

R.C.: It's very faint.

R.B.: Pardon?

R.C.: It's very faint.

R.B.: I can't hear you.

R.C.: Pardon?

R.B.: Try the other ear. (*R.C. covers it*): Now, what's that like?

R.C.: I still can't hear you.

R.B.: Can you hear me?

R.C.: Pardon?

R.B.: Hm. You definitely need a hearing-aid.

R.C.: I thought so.

R.B.: Pardon?

R.C.: You can't hear *me*, either, can you?

R.B.: Pardon?

R.C.: Why don't *you* wear one?

R.B.: You're still very faint.

R.C.: A HEARING-AID! Why don't *you* wear one?

R.B.: I *am* wearing one.

R.C.: Pardon?

R.B.: Pardon?

R.C.: I said, "Pardon?"

R.B.: Oh. I said, "Pardon!"

R.C.: Oh, never mind – I'll get some new teeth. (*He exits.*)

The RE

The living-room of the Colonel's residence — a stone's-throw from the barracks at Rawlpore, India. Time : 1894.

The room is overdressed, oppressive — above all, a feeling of heat. Insect noises. The distant cries of a Sergeant-Major, and men drilling, marching feet.

On the chaise longue, dressed from head to foot in white, or at most, off-white, lies the Colonel's lady. She reclines, fanning herself languidly. She is beautiful, thirty and very hot. Next to her, in a wider chair, sits the Colonel (R.B.). He is whiskered, dressed in full uniform, sixty, and sweating profusely. After a moment or two, he speaks.

COLONEL (*mopping his forehead*): Gad! The heat!

EDITH: It's the hot *season*.

COL: Yes — that's what does it. Phew! I hope it's not curry again tonight.

EDITH: It always is.

COL: The only thing they can make in this God-forsaken country. (*Pause*.) Would you like a whisky?

EDITH: Fire-water.

COL: Yes, quite. Tea?

EDITH: It takes two hours to get cool enough to drink.

COL: Fancy a game of cards?

Edith: It's too hot.

COL: There must be some little thing I can tempt you with.

EDITH: No — it's too hot for that, as well.

COL: True. Yes; thinking about it, I think you're right. Still, it's nice thinking about it. I think I'll have a gin. (*He rings handbell on table.*) Gad, the heat! Look at all this mess. (*Indicating drinking glasses, etc., on table.*) Damned filthy swine of a house-boy. Mahmud! Where the devil are you?

(*Enter an Indian house-boy, dressed in as little as possible within the convention of the period.*)

COL: Now look, here, you damned beggar, Colonel-massa want all-same great bit gin-tinkle, all-same full up top big big overflowing very little tonic water. You all-same lazybones, no sit about on big fat verandah, clear up all-same glasses in all-same living-hut or big Colonel-massa will all-same give you sack and big bag to put it in, understand? You all-same out on your big fat all-same ear! Savvy?

HOUSEBOY: (*shrugging*): It's all the same to me, dear. (*He minces out.*)

COL: We must be nearer the border than I thought! Damned cheeky swine! Thank God, Corporal Bligh is starting work here this afternoon. He should be here by now.

EDITH: Corporal Bligh?

COL: My batman. You remember him.

EDITH: Of *course* I do, George. I'm hardly likely to forget him. He undresses you every night in the bedroom.

COL: Oh, of course. Damned good batman, Bligh. Dashed keen.

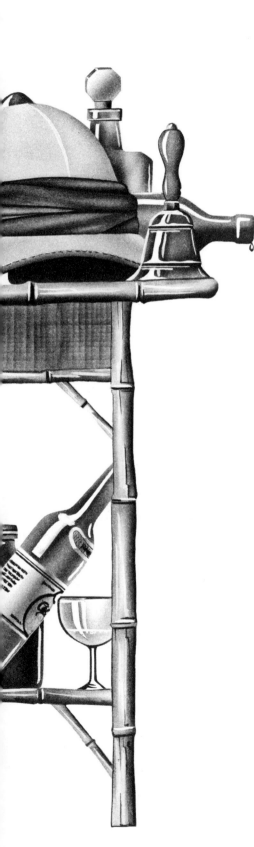

(*Door opens, and Corporal Bligh (R.C.) enters efficient, respectful, and breezy. The perfect gentleman's gentleman. He carries a glass of gin for the Colonel.*)

BLIGH: Good afternoon, sir – madam. Your gin, Colonel.

COL: Bligh! Good lad – you've arrived already. Splendid.

BLIGH: Yessir. Thought I'd pop over a bit early. Bit warmish today, sir.

COL: Warmish! I don't think I can stand it much longer. Gad! What must it be like for the lads on parade.

BLIGH: They'll stick it sir. It's the honour of the Regiment, sir.

COL: The Regiment. Yes. I must get out there, inspect them. Least I can do. (*Drinks gin.*) Where's my helmet? (*Picks up pith helmet.*) Gad, this thing weighs a ton – and it's too small (*which it is*). Can't something be done about it?

BLIGH: We could try taking the pith out of it, sir.

COL: Most of the chaps do that already. (*He exits.*)

(*Bligh sees Edith staring at him.*)

BLIGH: Everything to your satisfaction, madam?

(*Edith immediately grabs him with one arm and pulls him over the back of the chaise longue: he rolls on top of her – they finish up on the chaise, sitting, in an embrace.*)

EDITH: You *know* everything is NOT to my satisfaction, Corporal. Ever since that first accidental brush in the bedroom. It's all your fault, you wonderful creature.

BLIGH: That first accidental brush in the bedroom, as you put it, was *not* by fault, madam. I happened to be *using* the brush, but it was *you* who turned round quickly. There was little I could do.

EDITH: And you did it beautifully.

BLIGH: Well, that's as may be.

EDITH: There was no maybe about it. Kiss me.

BLIGH: But supposing the Colonel comes back and catches us?

EDITH: Let him.

BLIGH: But the honour of the Regiment!

EDITH: Damn the honour of the Regiment! What about my honour?

BLIGH: Ah, well, if you're going to start living in the past

EDITH (*she reacts*): It's the future I'm concerned with. The immediate future. Tonight?

BLIGH: Tonight? Where?

EDITH: In the clearing, where we met that evening. I'll never forget that first moment, when you came up behind me and grabbed me by the azaleas. Look at me! I'm trembling in your arms – my lips are burning, I've got pins and needles all up my back.

BLIGH: That's not passion, it's prickly heat. You ought to be lying down.

EDITH: That's what I keep telling you!

BLIGH: Look, madam, if you think I'm making love to you in broad daylight, you're mistaken.

EDITH: Let's go down into the cellar. (*She goes to the cellar door, opens it, and looks down.*) It's not broad daylight down there.

BLIGH: I'm sorry, but I'm not sinking to those sort of depths.

EDITH: It's quite a shallow cellar.

BLIGH: Nevertheless, I'm afraid it's beneath me. Gad, if only you weren't so beautiful – if only it weren't so hot!

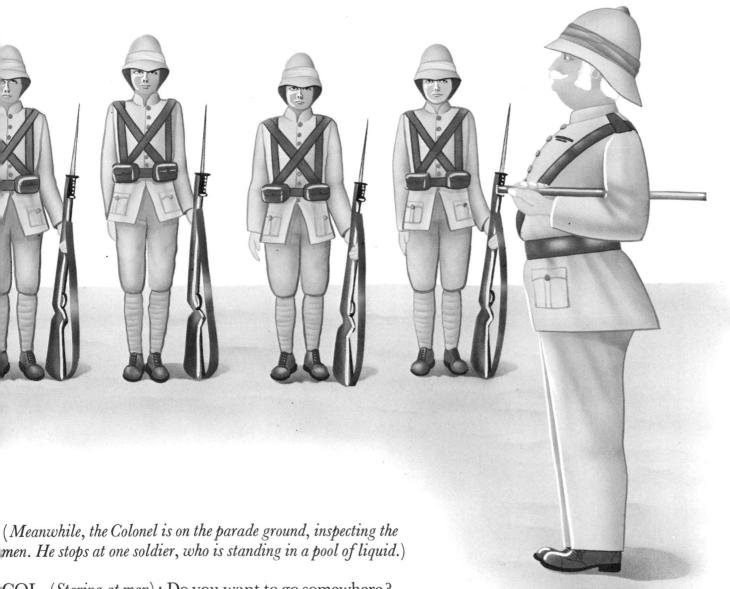

(*Meanwhile, the Colonel is on the parade ground, inspecting the men. He stops at one soldier, who is standing in a pool of liquid.*)

COL. (*Staring at man*): Do you want to go somewhere?

SOLDIER: Yes sir. Anywhere.

COL: What? (*To Sergeant.*) Is he all right?

SERGEANT: He sweats rather a lot, sir.

COL: Oh, I see. All right, men. In view of the extreme heat, you may all undo the top button of your tunic! (*The men begin to do this, gratefully. A cloud of steam rises all around them. The Colonel and the Sergeant exchange a look, and mop their brows.*)

(*In the bungalow, things are progressing. Edith, now without her dress, in white corset, bloomers above the knee, black stockings, bare shoulders, is smouldering on the sofa. Bligh stands by the door.*)

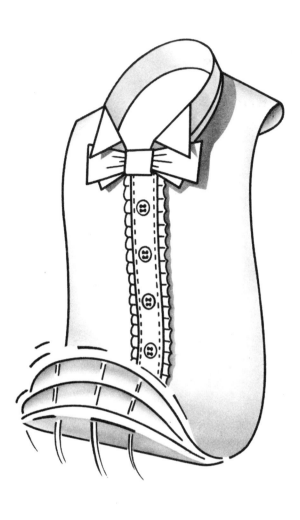

BLIGH: Look, I've *got* to go. I've got to starch the Colonel's front for tonight.

EDITH: Oh, very well. Go. But don't expect me to be any different when we next meet! I shall still want you desperately . . .

(*The Colonel enters ; luckily, Bligh is concealed from sight by the door, which opens onto him. As the Colonel moves towards Edith, Bligh slips out unseen. Edith, unaware, continues to declaim her love.*)

EDITH: I shall always want you. You did something to me then that no-one else has ever done. Not so violently, at any rate. You awakened something in me – something which had been lying dormant since I was a young, frightened girl at her first hunt-ball. There's been a lot of hunt-balls since then. But never any quite like the first. And so it was with you – I've never known anything that has moved me so much – or so often.

COL (*now on his own by the door*) : What the devil are you on about, old thing ?

EDITH: Oh – I didn't hear you come in.

COL: Never moved you so much or so often ? Sounds like an advert for Pickfords.

EDITH: I'm sorry, I was rambling. I think I'm out of my mind.

COL: Nonsense. Talking of being out of things, what happened to your dress ?

EDITH: I took it off. It's this accursed heat!

COL: I know. That's what drives a man mad. The heat. Like that chap that disappeared last month. Captain Wilcox, the Professor, they called him. Mad as a hatter, through the heat.

EDITH: What happened to him ?

COL: Just vanished overnight. Took two hundred feet of

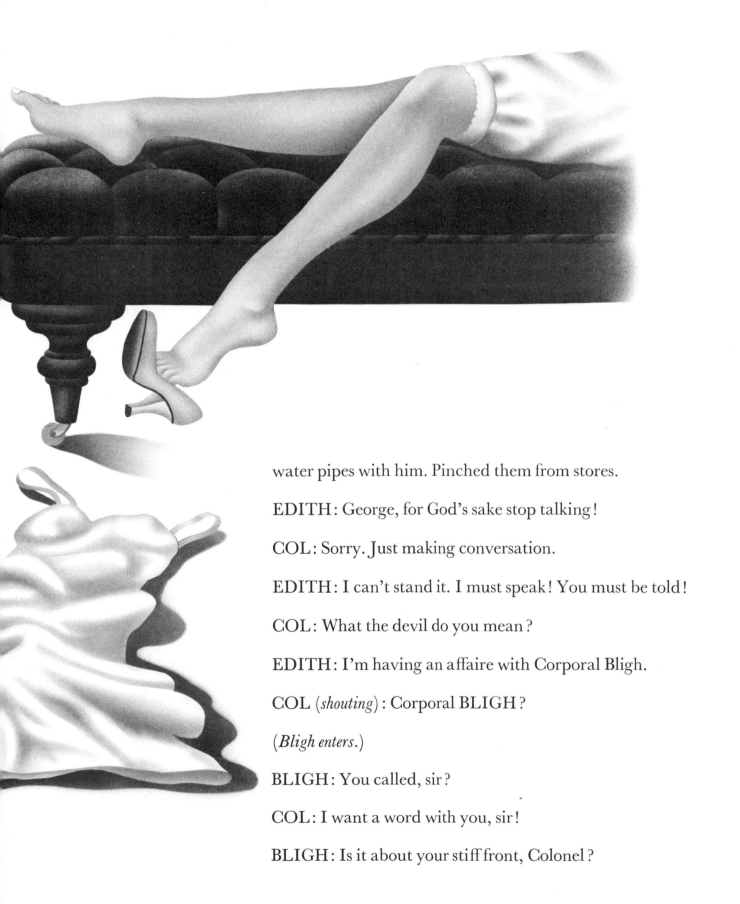

water pipes with him. Pinched them from stores.

EDITH: George, for God's sake stop talking!

COL: Sorry. Just making conversation.

EDITH: I can't stand it. I must speak! You must be told!

COL: What the devil do you mean?

EDITH: I'm having an affaire with Corporal Bligh.

COL (*shouting*): Corporal BLIGH?

(*Bligh enters.*)

BLIGH: You called, sir?

COL: I want a word with you, sir!

BLIGH: Is it about your stiff front, Colonel?

COL: No it's *not* about my stiff front, Corporal Bligh. Is it true, about you and Edith here?

BLIGH: Well, perhaps. I suppose you could think that. Is *what* true, sir?

COL: That you've had an affaire with her. Is it all true? That you've caressed her, touched her, fondled her, kissed her?

BLIGH: Well – only bits sir.

COL: Which bits? Point them out!

EDITH: George! Please!

COL: I'm going to fight you, sir. (*He starts to take off his coat.*) For the honour of the Regiment. I may be twice as old, but what I give away in age, I make up for in weight.

BLIGH: At least.

COL: Come on, put 'em up. (*He adopts a fighting attitude.*)

BLIGH (*takes off coat*): Very well, Colonel – but only for the Regiment.

(*A distant banging is heard. A sort of booming thud. The men look at each other.*)

COL: Wait a minute! Gunfire! An attack!

BLIGH: That's not guns, Colonel. That sounds as if it's coming from the cellar.

COL (*listens at cellar door*): You're right! (*Picks up large knobkerry or Indian club as weapon. The cellar door opens – and there enters a mad-eyed, bearded, straggly-haired man in a filthy tattered Captain's uniform. He is on the verge of collapse. He carries a piece of iron pipe*).

COL: Good God. So that's it! You remember the Professor, who disappeared with the water pipes?

WILCOX: I knew I could do it. It was all in my head!

BLIGH: Captain Wilcox!

COL: He's been down there for a month. No wonder we've
been so damned hot. Damn fool's gone and invented
central heating!

(*Edith faints, as the Professor dances about, half collapsing, and
the Colonel and Bligh restrain him. The parade ground band, in the
distance strikes up the Regimental march.*)

First Visit

A Doctor's waiting room. R.C. and R.B. are reading newspapers –
The Times *and* Jewish Chronicle *respectively.*

R.B.: Excuse me for interrupting you.

R.C.: Yes.

R.B.: This doctor – I've never been to him before – is he a
specialist?

R.C.: Oh yes, specialises in everything.

R.B.: Really? That's interesting. Tell me – er – is he expensive?

R.C.: Well, he is and he isn't. He charges you a hundred
guineas for the first visit.

R.B.: A HUNDRED GUINEAS?

R.C.: Ah, yes – but after that, all your visits are free – forever.

R.B.: You mean – no matter how many times you come and see
him, he doesn't charge you?

R.C.: Not after the first time, no.

R.B.: Oh, really? (*Nurse or Receptionist comes out of door.*)

NURSE: Mr. Greenbaum, please.

R.B. (*entering the door*): Hello doctor. Here I am again!

Phoney

A man in a phone box, dialling. A female voice answers.

Female Voice: Number please?

Man: Is that Interpol?

Female: This is the exchange, sir. What number did you require?

Man: Interpol. I want to speak to Interpol.

Female: Hold the line, sir.
(*A pause – buzzing and clicking.*)

Police Voice: Wandsworth police station. Can I help you, sir?

Man: I want Interpol, please.

P.C.: I'll connect you with Scotland Yard, sir. Hold on. (*More clicking.*)

Scotland Yard Voice: Scotland Yard here. Who do you wish to speak to, sir?

Man: Interpol.

Scotland Yard: Is it priority, sir?

Man: Er – yes, please.

Scotland Yard: Hold the line, please. (*More clicking.*)

Interpol Voice: Hello. Interpol here.

Man: Oh, Interpol? I want to send some flowers by wire to my mother.

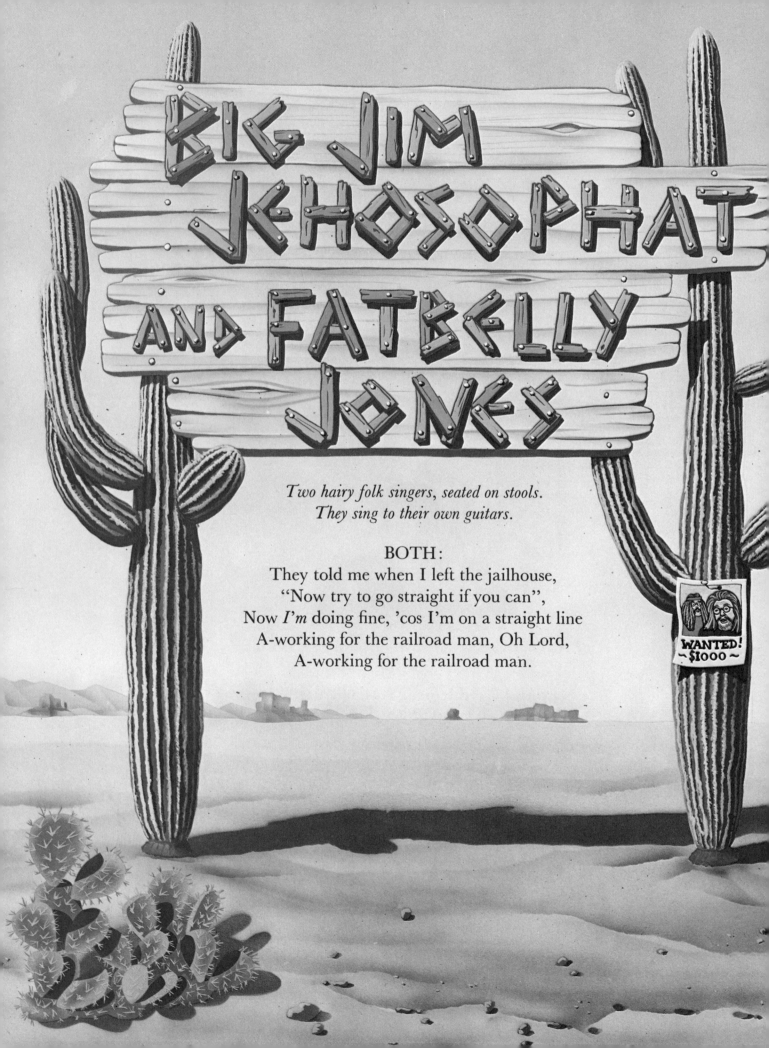

BIG JIM JEHOSOPHAT AND FATBELLY JONES

Two hairy folk singers, seated on stools.
They sing to their own guitars.

BOTH:
They told me when I left the jailhouse,
"Now try to go straight if you can",
Now *I'm* doing fine, 'cos I'm on a straight line
A-working for the railroad man, Oh Lord,
A-working for the railroad man.

WANTED!
~ $1000 ~

R.C.:

Oh, I crouched all night laying track down
And the wind on my back made me choke
And I felt that the bottom had fell out o' my life
Till I found that my braces had broke, Oh Lord,
I found that my braces had broke.

R.B.:

Someone has stole my hammer,
But I still got to earn my bread
And life ain't so grand, when you're standing on your hands,
And driving in the rivets with your head, Oh Lord,
And driving in the rivets with your head.

BOTH:

There's a curve in the track up yonder
I think it's the beginning of the end;
I've tried going straight, but sad to relate
I think I'm a'going round the bend, Oh Lord,
I think I'm a'going round the bend.

R.C.: Hi there, lovely people – it sure is a downright treat to be with you again – ain't that right, Fatbelly?

R.B.: Sure is, Big Jim.

R.C.: My buddy, ladies and gentlemen – Fatbelly Jones.

(*Applause*)

R.B.: Hello, people.

R.C.: Yessir, it's always a privilege to be allowed into your homes like this. Fatbelly here, course, he's been in more homes than I have, ain't you.

R.B.: That's right, Jim. I just come out of one last week.

R.C.: You better?

R.B.: Sure 'nuff Jim, yeah. I'm not right, but I'm better.

R.C.: Course, travelling around the countryside, as we do, not doing a regular job, just getting our food and shelter where we can, well, that kinda affects you, you know, good people. A strange feeling comes over you – a pleasant, unworldly calm settles upon your soul. And we have a name for it in the folk world. We call it – laziness.

R.B.: I love being lazy – I really work at it.

R.C.: Now, we've just sung you a work song, and now we're going to sing you a love song. 'Cos love and work, they're the really big things in people's lives, ain't they? I mean what else is there?

R.B.: Food.

R.C.: Yeah, we tried that one time. Fatbelly wrote a song about food once. What was it called, Fatbelly?

R.B.: "I'm in love with a big red jelly". Never caught on, though.

R.C.: No, certainly didn't. Boy, was that a lulu. (*Chuckling.*) People didn't know whether to sing it, eat it, or throw it in the fan. Anyways, here's a song – and Fatbelly here has got a new instrument he's just invented – show the good people your new instrument, Fat.

R.B.: There we are, Big Jim. (*He produces a stick with motor horns and whizzers and rattles on it.*)

R.C.: My, that's a mighty strange piece of equipment you got there, boy.

R.B.: Thanks, Big Jim.

R.C.: What do you call it?

R.B.: Well, I don't rightly call it anything, Big Jim; but I suppose if I *was* to call it anything, I guess I'd call it Norman.

R.C.: Why Norman?

R.B.: It's my favourite name.

R.C.: Yes, but that's for a *man*.

R.B.: No, no – I like women too, if they're called Norman.

R.C.: You're right, you *ain't* right, are you? O.K. let's hit the song. "The gell that's gonna marry me".

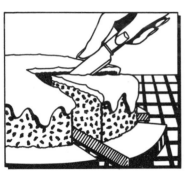   

BOTH: She can sow, she can hoe,
She can read, she can write,
She can cook a man a breakfast in the middle of the night,
She can cut up a chicken,
She can cut down a tree,
Wow! That's the gal who's gonna marry me.

She can dig, she can jig,
She can juggle, she can jump,
She can drive a fella crazy with a wiggle of her rump,
She can stand in the saddle,
She can sit on your knee,
Wow! That's the girl who's gonna marry me.

She can joke, she can smoke,
She can drink a dozen beers,
She can move a grand pianner, she can move a man to tears,
She can pour out her heart or
She can pour out your tea,
Yep! That's the gal who's gonna marry me.

She can roast, she can toast,
She can boil, she can bake,
She can cut a fella dead and she can cut a slice of cake,
She can cook a fella's goose and
She can fry a fricassee,
Yep! That's the gal who's gonna marry me.

She can sweep, she can weep,
She can giggle, she can grin,
She can play a little poker, and she can play a little gin,
She's as spicy as a pickle
And sweeter than a pea,
Hup! She's the gal who's gonna marry me.

R.C.   Well, now, just about time to leave you dear kind sweet ugly people, and Fatbelly and I just want you to know how grateful we are for you inviting us into your homes like this, don't we Fatbelly?

R.B.:   Anything you say, Jim.

R.C.:   Right on. We're going to find a more serious note to end on.

R.B.:   E flat's a good one.

R.C.:   We'll leave you now with our latest number, "Blows my mind".
Bye now!

BOTH:
The river's flowing up the hill,
It keeps moving I keep still,
Some folks say that thinking makes you blind
And when the wind is blowing from behind
It blows my mind.

Painted girls and neon light,
Lord you made the darkness bright,
The hole in my blue jeans is hard to find
But when the wind is blowing from behind
It blows my mind.

I'll go home and change my clothes,
Brush my hair and blow my nose,
A barrel-organ's life is one long grind
And when the wind is blowing from behind
It blows my mind.

(The lights fade and the camera zooms back.
The two hairy figures dwindle away
into the darkness.)

41

A Clinic In Limerick

The scene is a waiting room. A patient enters, bent double.
He hobbles over to a notice on the wall, and reads aloud.

Consultant, R. KELLY, M.D.
Assistant, J. LONG, Ph.D.

Please hang up your coat,
For ear, nose and throat.
For a blister, see Sister.

Nurse (*entering*):   That's me.
                        I take it you have an appointment?

Patient: I was just bending down, and this joint went
                at the back of my thigh. I was just passing by . . .

Nurse: Step through here, and I'll rub on some ointment.

Patient: No, I'll just wait and see Doctor Smithers.

Nurse: I'm afraid he is no longer with us.

Patient: Oh, a new one, eh? Nice?

Nurse: Well, his hands are like ice. And while
                you're undressing, he dithers.

Patient: I've begun to feel weak at the knees.

Doctor (*over intercom.*):   Will you send in the next patient, please.

Nurse: In you go. Be a man! (*As the patient goes to door.*)
                I'll just switch off that fan —
                When you're stripped, there's a terrible breeze.

                (*They both pass through into the consulting room.*)

Doctor: Lord save us! He hops like a rabbit!
                Grab my arm — come on man, I said grab it!

(The patient tries – the Doctor pushes him in the back, trying to straighten him out.)

Doctor: Well. We'd best oil the springs. Come on
take off your things.

(The nurse removes her uniform in one zipping movement.)

Doctor: Not *you*, nurse!

Nurse: I'm sorry – just habit.

(She picks up her uniform, and goes out.)

Doctor: My name's Doctor Kelly – sit down. Oh, you
can't – never mind, Mr. . . .

Patient: Crown.

Doctor: Just go round by the screen.

(They go behind a screen – patient cannot be seen, because he is bent over, but Doctor can.)

Doctor: Now then, what's to be seen? Had your holidays
yet? Aren't you brown! Oh my gosh – hold
your breath – grit your teeth! Your braces are
caught underneath. Well, you *are* in a state –
we were almost too late. If they'd snapped,
you'd have needed a wreath. Now, there's one
way to make you unbend –

(He brandishes a large pair of scissors, then disappears behind screen.)

Patient: Ow, my . . . *(TWANG! go the braces.)*

Doctor: There, you're cured, my friend –
I'm a Limerick man; I make sure, if I can
that you get the joke right in the end!

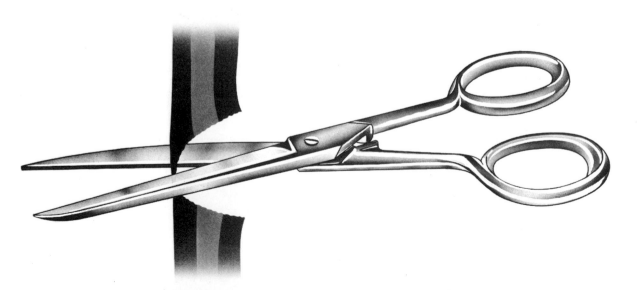

THE CASE
OF MRS. MACE

A Police Station – a room or office within the Station itself. R.B. as plain-clothes North Country detective, sits at a desk. R.C. enters.

R.C.: Good day, Inspector Jay.

R.B.: Morning, Dorning. Any news of the Girder murder?

R.C.: Yessir. He's been shot at Oxshott. Bagshot got him with a slingshot full of buckshot.

R.B.: He's a good shot, Bagshott. Well, you must be pleased *that* situation's eased.

R.C.: The relief is beyond belief, chief. My mind is once more a blank. And I've only you to thank.

R.B.: All right. Never mind the fawning, Dorning. I'm glad to hear your head's clear: it means there's more space for the Mrs. Mace case to take its place.

R.C.: The Mrs. Mace case? Have they traced the face? (*Points to photofit blow-up on wall*).

R.B.: No – and the nightdress is still missing.

R.C.: Is she sure it was the right nightdress? She's not mistaken about what was taken?

R.B.: How come, little chum?

R.C.: Well, to the voluptuous Mrs. Mace, all her nightdresses are equally seductively attractive and attractively seductive. Whatever she wore, she'd still be a bountiful, beautiful nightie-full.

R.B.: She's certainly a grand lady to have as a landlady. I've been told, that her teapot's *never* cold.

R.C.: I'd be delighted to be selected to inspect her inspector. Any prospects of any suspects?

R.B.: Yes – two. Two of them are actors who lodge with Grace – Mrs. Mace, at her place in the Chase. Leo Mighty, the leading man, known for his portrayals of charmers, farmers and men in pyjamas. And the other one is Roger Mainger, the stage manager, who once played a mad stranger in a film starring Stewart Granger called "Deadly Danger".

R.C.: May I add another to your list? If I'm not being too bumptious or presumpteous?

R.B.: Who?

R.C.: Sergeant Bodger!

R.B.: What? That replacement constable from Dunstable. You must be crazy.

R.C.: It's just a theory, dearie. May I sit down?

R.B.: Please – make yourself comfy, Humphrey.

(*R.C. sits.*)

R.C.: It's just that Bodger has got a face like a fit: which fits the face on the Photofit in the first place, and he's often to be found at her place, in the Chase, filling his face with fish.

R.B.: Fish?

R.C.: Fried by Grace – Mrs. Mace. Mostly dace – or plaice.

R.B.: But what about Leo Mighty? He's there nightly – isn't it slightly more likely? She obviously looks very flighty in her nightie – he's the sort of toff that might try to pull it off.

R.C.: Possibly – but here's something you don't know.

R.B.: I don't?

R.C.: No. I've spoken with Roger.

R.B.: Roger?

R.C.: The lodger.

R.B.: Oh – Roger Mainger, who played the stranger with Granger.

R.C.: He says he saw Leo take the nightgown. He was staring through the keyhole in Mrs. Mace's bedroom door.

R.B.: He dared to stare through there? Would he swear he saw Leo Mighty take the nightie?

R.C.: He'll do plenty of swearing. No wonder he was staring – it was the one she was wearing!

R.B.: What? Surely not!

R.C.: He stood on the bed, and pulled it over her head. She went red, and he fled. He locked himself in the shed, and wished he were dead. She was going to phone her cousin Ted, but felt dizzy in the head, so she lay on the bed instead, and went red.

R.B.: So you said. Roger is a liar!

R.C.: Have you any proof, you old poof?

R.B.: I've seen where Mrs. Mace sleeps. It's an attic! So the story about pulling the garment over her head is false. He would have to pull the nightgown right down! There's no headroom in her bedroom!

R.C.: So Roger's lying! Then he must be the culprit! Game set and match, chief! And so ends the disgraceful Grace Mace case.

R.B.: (*picks up the phone*) : I'll just tell the Chief Constable – what a relief, constable. (*Into phone*) Hello, sir – we've solved the Mace case. I'm happy to tell you that Leo is innocent, and so is Sergeant Bodger. Yes, sir; in other words – 'twas not Leo Mighty who lifted the nightie, 'twas Roger the Lodger, the soft-footed dodger, and not Sergeant Bodger, thank God!

AN APPEAL — FOR WOMEN

A man with a moustache at a desk.

R.B.: Good evening. My name is Arnold Splint, and I am here tonight. (*A caption appears on the screen saying "AN APPEAL – FOR WOMEN"*). This is an appeal for women only. No, please don't switch off – because it's you men I want to talk to especially tonight. I am appealing to you, for women. I need them desperately. I can't get enough – and the reason I'm appealing to you men, is that I don't appeal to women. But I still need them. So this is how you can help. If you have any old women you no longer need – send her to me. Simply tie her arms and legs together, wrap her in brown paper and post her to me, care of the B.B.C., with your own name printed clearly on the bottom. Because that's the bit I shall undo first. Of course, I cannot guarantee to make use of all women sent to me. It depends on the condition, so make sure you enclose a stamped addressed pair of knickers.

Send as many women as you like – no matter how small. I assure you, all those accepted will be made good use of by me

and my team of helpers – who, incidentally, carry on this work,
many without any form of support. I do hope you can find time
to send me something: we did originally start collecting with a
a van, from door to door, but this scheme was abandoned,
owing to wear and tear on the knockers.

I think we should remember, that Xmas is on its way. And when
it comes, and you are sitting at home, by your own fireside,
warming yourself beside a roaring great woman, think of all
those poor unfortunate people who are having to go without
this Xmas. Why not send them an old flame or two, to warm the
cockles of their hearthrug? I'm quite sure that many of you
have women lying about in drawers, that you haven't touched
for years. Please, post them off today. Help us set up our
Women on Wheels service for old men who can't move about. I
know it's not easy. It requires self-denial, patience, and an
enormous amount of string; but I'm sure you'll feel better for it.
I know I shall. Good night.

COLDITZ

Scene 1 THE ARRIVAL

The Castle yard. Two men are throwing a ball to each other, others are sitting in a circle, talking. The sound of a lorry is heard, it stops, the four guards get out of the back, escorting R.C. as the R.A.F. Air-Gunner, as played by David McCallum: with the pencil moustache and ruffled hair.

R.C.: So this is Colditz. They'll never keep *me* in here!

(*They march him away round a corner, out of sight. Round the corner they come into view. R.C., however, isn't with them, they realise this, and the captain cries, "Halt". They run back round the corner. The group is seated there, still chatting. The Germans look suspiciously at them. Then a guard points, and we see R.C. walking away in the middle distance. He has his trousers rolled up, his jacket tied round his waist like a skirt, his scarf tied round his head, and he carries a bucket and broom. He looks from the back like an old charwoman: but we know it's him. The guards run after him, and grab him.*)

R.C.: Just testing you.

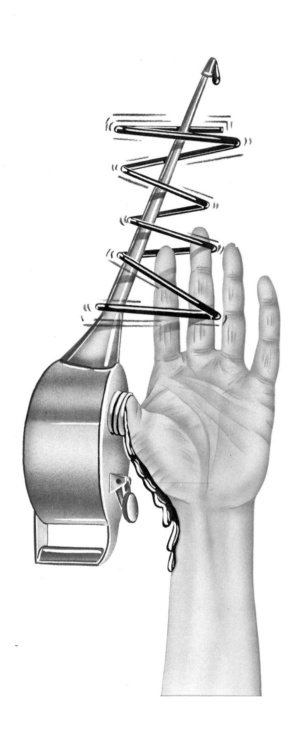

Scene 2 THE DORM

The prisoners' dormitory — or rather, a corner of it — next to the latrines. Two-tier wooden bunks, etc. On one of these lies Chapman, a prisoner, tall, thin. Perhaps two others, reading, also two chaps throwing a ball to each other.

R.C. is brought in by a guard named Helmut. Chapman gets up to greet him.

CHAPMAN: Hello there.

R.C.: My name's Carter. George Carter. (*Shaking hands.*) How are you?

CHAP: I'm Dicky.

R.C.: I don't feel so good myself. How long have you been here?

CHAP: Four years.

R.C.: Four years, cooped up here? No wonder you're feeling dicky. Haven't you tried to escape?

CHAP: My *name's* Dicky.

R.C.: Oh, I see.

CHAP: And don't think you're going to escape from here. The place, is impregnable.

R.C.: Don't you believe it, chum. That's what they said about Doreen Phipps. How wrong they were!

CHAP: Were they?

R.C.: Well, I'm paying her thirty bob a week, judge for yourself. (*He moves around, sizing the place up.*) No, we'll soon be out of here.

CHAP: You better have a word with Captain Whitmore.

R.C.: Where is he?

CHAP: I'm not sure, I . . .

(*There is a banging inside one of the latrines.*)

R.B. (*inside the loo*) : Anybody there? I'm stuck. The door's jammed. Hello! (*Etc. as he bangs on the door.*)

CHAP: That's him. (*Calling.*) Coming!

(*They eventually succeed in prising open the latrine door. R.B. comes out dressed as Army Captain.*)

R.B.: How do you do – Whitmore. I'm the escape officer.

R.C.: Carter, sir.

(*R.C. salutes. R.B. salutes back – he has an oil can stuck onto his little finger.*)

R.B.: Sorry about the oil can. Can't get my finger out. Got it stuck. Trying to oil my bed-springs.

R.C.: Really sir? Is this a mixed dormitory then?

R.B.: Oh, yes, rather. Officers *and* men.

R.C.: Oh. I see. Right, that does it. I'm getting out of here.

R.B.: Now listen, Carter. Sit down. It's not as easy as all that. We have a code of conduct in here. Of *course*, you want to escape. Everybody does. But it has to be organised. You need papers. Money. Clothing, a cover story. And this means none of this "go it alone" stuff. We've built up a specialised team to deal with every aspect, and each escape has to be planned. Planned down to the very last detail, do you understand?

(*The door is opened by a guard. R.B., immediately ignoring his own advice, tries to rush out. A pathetic attempt, which fails dismally. R.C. reacts in contempt.*)

Scene 3 THE ESCAPE BEGINS

The dormitory is in semi-darkness. The alsatians howl. R.B. as Whitmore with Chapman, sit on bottom bunk. Two other prisoners are throwing a ball to each other.

CHAP: Ssh! I think he's coming back.

R.B.: Is that you, Carter? How's it going?

R.C. (*emerging from under bed*): Pretty good. Another couple of feet. (*He hands R.B. two socks, full of earth.*)

R.B.: Oh, thanks. How much further to go?

R.C.: I've just told you, two more feet.

R.B.: Oh, I see – I thought you meant these. (*Indicating socks.*) Here you are, Chapman. (*Gives socks to Chapman, who empties the earth into the drawer of his locker.*)

CHAP (*as he does so*): Isn't it someone else's turn to provide the socks? (*As he puts sock on his foot.*) What about you, Whitmore?

R.B.: I've got a potato in mine.

CHAP: I shall be able to grow them in mine if this goes on.

(*Suddenly everyone pretends to be doing something else, as marching feet approach. The door opens, and in comes the Matron, a large curvy blonde, all knickers and knockers, as they say. But a wonderful actress.*)

R.B.: Evening, Matron.

MATRON: Good evening Vitmore, Chepman. I am happy to inform you that the R.A.F. have dropped a load of Red Cross parcels for you.

R.B.: Marvellous!

MATRON: Unfortunately, when they hit the ground they were flattened completely. Only one survived.

R.B.: How?

MATRON: I was sunbathing on the roof and it landed right on top of me. It bounced.

R.B.: It would.

MATRON: Bring it in please. (*a guard brings in the box.*)

R.B. (*opening it*): Oh, well, that explains it. It's a load of balls. (*He takes out a rubber ball. The Matron eyes him, and exits briskly.*)

R.C.: Right, lads. This is it. I'm going to make my final bid for freedom. If I'm not back in three hours, come through the tunnel and investigate.

CHAP: Good luck, Carter – drop us a postcard!

R.C.: I'll do better than that. As soon as I get to France, I'll send you a letter. 'Bye skipper. (*R.B. and R.C. shake hands and R.C. disappears under the bed.*)

R.B.: Well, now all we have to do is wait.

(*Cut to a clock on the locker. The hands whizz round from six o'clock to nine o'clock. A caption appears: "THREE HOURS LATER".*)

R.B.: Well, it's three hours later. I'm going through to investigate. (*He crawls under the bed.*)

(*A close up of a cupboard. The door opens, R.B. crawls out, dusty. He stands up, and stares.*)

R.B.: Good Lord!

(*Cut to R.C. and Matron, on top of bed. Suspenders in evidence; especially hers. We are in Matron's bedroom.*)

R.B.: What are you doing!

R.C.: You've got to take it where you can get it.

R.B.: You never told me the tunnel came out in Matron's room.

R.C.: Pure coincidence. Bit of luck, though, wasn't it?

Scene 4 THE DORM AGAIN

Three days later, in the dormitory. The final escape bid is about to begin. R.B. and R.C. in same clothes, but blackened faces, a la commandoes. Chapman is with them.

R.C.: This time it's got to work.

R.B.: Don't see why it shouldn't. We've got papers, money. Once we get over that wall, we stand a damn good chance.

CHAP: Got the sheets tied together?

R.C.: Only two. Most of the chaps have been damn mean about parting with their sheets. Selfish baskets. You were the only one who volunteered.

CHAP: That's all right.

R.B.: Just two sheets, eh? How high's the wall.

CHAP: Eighty feet.

R.B.: Hm. Just have to drop the last bit. Right, come on then. (*To Chapman.*), Bye, Chapman, old sport. See you after the war. (*Opens the door.*) All clear.

R.C.: Cheerio, Dicky. And thanks again for the sheets. (*He goes.*)

CHAP: 'Bye. (*Closes the door and goes over to the bunk bed.*) Who needs sheets? (*Calling under bed.*) Coming, Matron!

(*He begins to climb into the tunnel under the bed.*)

TO THE GROUND
60 FEET

Scene 5 THE ESCAPE

R.C. and R.B. with blackened faces – scurrying here and there, climbing, listening etc. The usual shot of attacking a guard and overpowering him – lots of mood music and sound effects. Finally, R.B. and R.C. look down over the eighty foot wall. They throw over their short sheets, slide down and drop about sixty feet onto the grass. Amazingly, they stagger to their feet.

R.C.: Well, we're over. You all right?

R.B.: Bit of a headache. Now, I suggest we stay put under the shadow of the wall until the morning.

R.C.: Good idea. (*He puts a blanket round their knees as they huddle together for warmth.*) Good night, Whitmore.

R.B.: 'Night, old boy.

(*They close their eyes.*)

Scene 6 THE AWAKENING

The early morning sun casts long shadows. Our heroes are still asleep against the wall. Shouting can be heard in the distance. A shadow looms over them suddenly. It wears a peaked cap. We hear its voice; rasping, Germanic.

Voice: Good morning, gentlemen. So, you got over the wall, did you? (*They start to stir, and open their eyes.*) You will be sorry, I can assure you. (*They stare up in dismay at the man in the peaked cap.*) Velcome to Butlitz.

(*Now at last, a shot of the scene: it is Butlitz holiday camp. The man wears a striped blazer, white trousers and a coloured peak cap. Holiday-makers stroll about. We do not, however, linger on the scene for too long, but zoom in dramatically to the barbed wire on the top of the fence, as the word "BUTLITZ" in heavy German lettering, fills the screen.*)

*A glittering stage. A voice is heard, "Ladies and
Gentlemen – it's the Short and Fat Minstrel Show!" R.B.
and R.C. blacked-up, enter, accompanied by other short and
fat minstrels, and short and fat showgirls.*

They all burst into the first chorus of "Robert E. Lee".

Fat Men: See them shuffling along,
            Hear them singing this song
            Just bring a big pal

A fat gal,
If she's fat and heavy
Get down on the levee.

Short Men: Will you let those little gals through
And if they're very small, we'll take two.

All: We're short and fat, but,
That don't stop us singing,
All these songs we're bringing to you.

SWANEE RIVER

R.B.:
Way down upon the Swanee River
I met Kat Maguire,
Two onions and a pound of liver,
That's how she won my desire.

She knew just how to cook my dinner,
Oh! Shut my mouth -
No chance of ever getting thinner
Down in the deep-fried South.

All the steaks were rich and fatty
All the beans were tinned,
That's why my heart is burning ever
That's why I'm gone with the wind.

SWING LOW SWEET CHARIOT

R.C.:
I looked 'cross the water, and what did I see
Standing on the sea-front at Frome?
A gal with a bust that measured fifty-three
Looked like St. Peter's in Rome.

Her name was Harriet -
A stripper at the Hipperdrome,
Swing low, sweet Harriet
Took four men to carry her home.

THE GIRL I LEFT BEHIND ME

R.B.:
Oh, I'm in love with Abigail
And her shape is most unusual,
She's put the whole lot up for sale
And I've got first refusal.

THE MAN I LOVE

R.B.: Oh, he's so short and fat – the man I love:
He's such a little sprat – the man I love:
He's knee-high to a gnat
And that is that –
But he's – my man.

He wears a trilby hat – the man I love
And he's a bit "like that" – the man I love
He ain't no acrobat
Trips on the cat
But he's – my man.

Though he sets my heart on fire
He's a liar, goodness knows,
Though he often says we're through, dear
When he says "so long" it's never true, dear.

Last night the diamond pin
In his cravat
It pierced my blown-up bra,
And left me flat
I guess you'd say that that
Was Tit-for-Tat
The man I love.

I Dream Of Jeannie

R.C.:
I dream of Jeannie with the bright pink hair,
She's had it dyed to match her underwear,
I dream of Mary with the big red nose
Wonder if she wears red flannel underclothes,
Then I dream of purple ones, those pretty ones of Heather's,
Then I dream of Polly, who covers hers with feathers,
I dream of Daisy May, who works at the vicar's
Daisy drives me cray-hay-zee, without any trouble.

POLLY WOLLY-DOODLE

R.B.: Now my little sister Polly
She is really very jolly
She went out and bought a dog the other day
It's a poodle that is woolly
And she pulls it on a pulley
Singing Polly's woolly poodle all the day.
People popped into the parlour
To see Polly's woolly Poodle
With a bowl of chicken noodle on a tray
Saying, "Polly, dear, this food'll
Please your pretty little poodle,"
She was popular with people right away.
Sad to say
Came the day
Polly's reputation fell completely flat
When the parson and his daughters
Sang "The parting of the waters"
Polly's poodle did a puddle on the mat.

SWANEE

R.B.:   Ronnie, how I envy, how I envy
Dear little Ronnie
I'd give the world to be
Just like young R.C.
Six stone four and five foot three
But Mammy's
Waiting for me
Cooking for me
Spuds and spaghetti
You'll find the jokes ain't
Funny no more
When you're stuck in the pantry door.

R.C.:   Ronnie, how I envy, how I envy
Dear, big, fat Ronnie
If only I had grown
I'd be so full-blown
Eighteen stone of skin and bone
And fat that
Keeps you cosy
Warm and rosy
When the nights are chilly
I'd be a great big
Crowd on my own
If only I was eighteen stone.

All
(*with Choir*):   Swanee, how I love yah, how I love yah
My dear old Swanee!

R.C. & R.B.   The folks at home will be
(*with Choir*):   So glad to know, we're
Working at the B.B.C.-ing you, next
Week, if they'll allow us to come back
On the telly—
So once again, we'll
Say cheerio,

All: The short and fat Minstrel Show!

A WEDDING SERVICE

The Bridegroom waits. The Wedding March is played as the Bride approaches on the arm of her father, followed by little girl bridesmaids. The Vicar stands facing them. The Bride arrives, the music stops, and she lifts her veil, eyes downcast.

VICAR: Dearly beloved, we are gathered here, in the face of this congregation, to join together this man and this woman . . .

MAN (*staring at woman, then addressing Vicar in a whisper*):
        Er . . . Excuse me . . .

VICAR (*whispering*): What's the matter?

MAN: This isn't the one.

VICAR: Which one?

MAN: This one isn't. She's not the one I'm
         marrying.

VICAR: Not the one you're marrying?

MAN: No. (*To girl*) Are you? I've never seen her
         before. Have I?

GIRL (*shaking head nervously*): No.

VICAR: Are you sure?

MAN: Course I'm sure.

GIRL: Oh dear, everyone's looking at us.

VICAR: Well — what's gone wrong?

GIRL: Could you carry on with the service?
Everyone's listening.

VICAR: Well, I can hardly . . .

MAN: Yes, look, carry on for a minute while we have
a think.

VICAR: Oh, all right . . . which estate is not by any to be
enterprised, not taken in hand, inadvisedly,
lightly, or wantonly; but reverently, discreetly,
advisedly, and soberly — duly considering the
cause for which matrimony was ordained . . .
(*This is spoken under the following dialogue*) etc.,
etc.

GIRL: What are we going to do?

MAN: Well, it's obvious. We've got to stop it haven't
we? I mean . . .

GIRL: Oh, I *can't*. I *can't*. I've waited for months for
this moment. I've been working up to it.

MAN: Well, so have I. I mean — well we both have,
but we've been working up to it with different
people, haven't we?

GIRL: Yes, but my mum will go mad if we cancel it.
She's got all the sandwiches and sausage rolls
ready and everything — and she's doing little
things in vol-au-vent cases as well.

MAN: Yes, but marriage is not just a question of little
things in vol-au-vent cases, is it?

GIRL: She sat up all night in an armchair so she
wouldn't spoil her new hair-do. Anyway I don't
know what you're like, do I?

MAN: Well, I'm just like anybody else, aren't I?

GIRL: You're very little.

MAN: I'm not little. It's you that's big.

VICAR (*who has come to the end of his words*): Er – have you decided anything yet? Because I've come to the part where the whole thing tends to become a tiny bit irrevocable.

GIRL: Oh – it's just that we don't know whether we are suited. It's a question of size.

VICAR: May I remind you both that a marriage partner is usually taken on account of his quality, not quantity.

MAN: Well, you'll have to give us another minute somehow.

VICAR: Tell you what – I'll give them a hymn to be going on with. (*Aloud*) The congregation will now sing hymn number 798. "A stranger is amongst us, O shall we let him in".

(*The congregation starts to sing.*)

GIRL: Look, I don't mind short men.

MAN: Really? Matter of fact, I love tall girls.

GIRL: Do you? I'm not really tall, you know.

MAN: You are to me.

GIRL: Yes. (*A pause.*) What do you think then? Shall we make a go of it?

MAN: Where would we live?

GIRL: Oh, my dad's bought me a new bungalow.

MAN: Oh, well, that settles it, you're on. (*To Vicar.*)
          O.K. Reverend, you can carry on.

VICAR: Ah. We'll just wait until the hymn finishes.

MAN: Oh all right then. (*A pause.*) We *have* met before
          actually. At school.

GIRL: Go on! Were you at the same school?

MAN: We were in the same class.

VICAR (*declaring*): Do you, er . . . ?

MAN: Robin Cyril.

VICAR: Robin Cyril.

GIRL: Robin Bates!

VICAR: Do you, Robin Bates.

MAN: Robin Cyril.

VICAR: Robin Cyril, take . . .

GIRL: Old Mother Thompsons!

VICAR: Take Old Mother Thompson.

GIRL: Mavis Jean.

VICAR: Take Mavis Jean, to your lawful wedded wife –
          to have and to hold (*etc. under dialogue*) . . .

MAN: I always swore I'd marry you – ever since I was
          nine. I never thought it would turn out like
          this. (*In response to Vicar*) I do.

VICAR: And do you, Mavis Jean, take Robin Cyril
          (*etc . . .*)

MAN: Here – what about the bloke you were
          supposed to marry?

GIRL: Oh, I never liked him much. Anyway, he was only marrying me out of sympathy, really. (*To Vicar.*) I do.

VICAR: For as much as Robin Cyril and Mavis Jean have consented together (*etc . . .*)

MAN: What do you mean, sympathy?

GIRL: Well, he took advantage of me.

MAN: Oh. Oh, well, that can't be helped – doesn't mean to say you've got to marry him, does it?

GIRL: Well, I thought it only right – I mean . . .

VICAR: . . . I pronounce that they be man and wife together.

GIRL (*indicating six bridesmaids*): . . . I've got to give this lot a father, haven't I?

(*The Man faints flat on his back.*)

GENTLEMAN CALLER

An intruder stands there; a mild little man, with a holdall and a guilty expression.

HOUSEHOLDER (*seeing intruder*): Good God!

INTRUDER: Ah! You're in. Good.

HOUSEHOLDER: So are you, it seems. What are you doing in my dining room?

INTRUDER: Er – I'm – I'm . . . I'm just . . . Higgins. I'm just Higgins. Justin Higgins. Solicitor. Any soliciting today? I mean is there anything you want solicited?

HOUSEHOLDER: You're not a solicitor.

INTRUDER: I'm not a *good* solicitor; no. I'll be quite frank with you – I'm fairly rotten, as a solicitor. My partner deals with most of the legal work. I'm more the tree-lopping side of the business.

HOUSEHOLDER: You're the what?

INTRUDER: I lop trees. Got any trees want lopping? General garden work?

HOUSEHOLDER: What?

INTRUDER: Well, let's put it this way – how are you off for manure? Got plenty about the place, have you?

HOUSEHOLDER: I haven't got *any* about the place.

INTRUDER: Right. I'll put you down for a hundredweight. Now what about seeds? Plants for the garden?

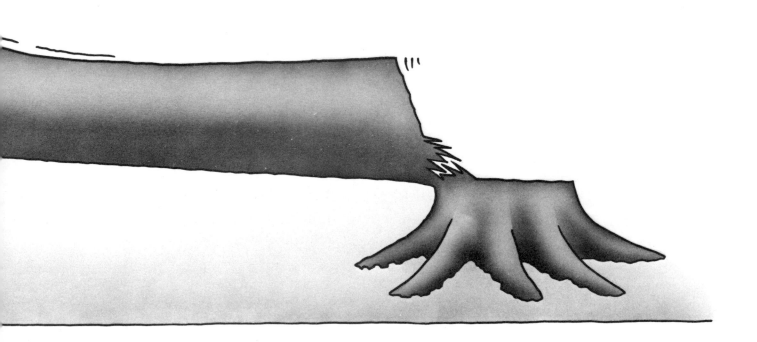

HOUSEHOLDER: Now just a minute!

INTRUDER (*attentively*): Just a minute, yes?

HOUSEHOLDER: This is a flat. And it's nine floors up.

INTRUDER: Well have you considered sunflowers? They're nice and tall. You could get the people downstairs to water them to start with, and then . . .

HOUSEHOLDER: You know nothing about gardening whatsoever.

INTRUDER: Oh, *don't* I?

HOUSEHOLDER: Well, do you?

INTRUDER: *I* don't; no. But my brother's wonderful. He's got green fingers.

HOUSEHOLDER: Oh, *he's* the gardener.

INTRUDER: No, he works in a trading stamp factory. But why I really came to see you, is, well, to put it frankly, doctor, it's this pain in my back . . .

HOUSEHOLDER: Listen! You're talking a lot of rubbish.

INTRUDER: The pain in my back *and* the pain in my head –

HOUSEHOLDER: You're a crook.

INTRUDER: Now steady on.

HOUSEHOLDER: What have you got in that bag?

INTRUDER: Er – sandwiches. Just my sandwiches for my lunch. One beef, and two cheese and chutney.

HOUSEHOLDER: In a bag that size?

INTRUDER: And a gallon of light ale.

HOUSEHOLDER: You're lying.

INTRUDER: Yes, I am.

HOUSEHOLDER: Oh, you admit it?

INTRUDER: Yes, I do.

HOUSEHOLDER: Ah!

INTRUDER: It's two beef and *one* cheese and chutney.

HOUSEHOLDER (*grabbing bag*):   Come on, let's have a look –

INTRUDER: How dare you! Leave that bag alone! Those sandwiches are private!

HOUSEHOLDER (*peering into bag*):   What's this? Books? Been stealing books from the bookshops eh?

INTRUDER: Certainly not. I've just been to the library.

HOUSEHOLDER: These are brand new!

INTRUDER: Yes. They're from the brand new library in Station Road.

HOUSEHOLDER (*reading*):   *The Home Encyclopedia.* Eight volumes, eh? I could do with a set of these.

INTRUDER: Well you're not having those. I took a lot of trouble pinch . . . borrowing those. They're very difficult to borrow, those are. They're fifteen quid a set in the shops, these are.

HOUSEHOLDER: Now look. Here's ten quid. Now either you take the money and clear off, or I shall pick up the 'phone and get the police. And that would put you *right* in it. Wouldn't it?

INTRUDER: Oh, that reminds me – do you want that hundredweight of manure or not?

HOUSEHOLDER: Come on, out! (*He propels him toward the door.*)

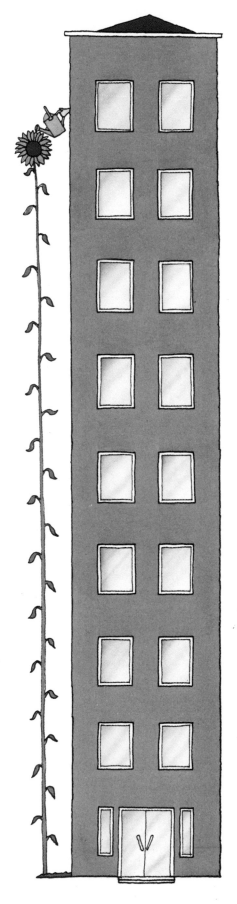

79

INTRUDER: You haven't heard the last of this! I'll get my brother on to you. (*He is pushed out of the door but pokes his head round again.*) Not the one with green fingers, the solicitor one!

HOUSEHOLDER: Out! (*Moving slowly away.*) Or I'll 'phone the police.

INTRUDER: All right – I'm going.

(*The door is slammed in his face. Outside the door a younger man is leaning against the wall.*)

YOUNG MAN: How d'you get on, Jack?

INTRUDER: All right Harry. Sold another set.

RAILWAY PLATFORM

A country station platform. R.C. and R.B. meet. They are dressed as conventional stuffy Englishmen. Each carries a weekend case or holdall.

R.C.: Hello, Ted.

R.B.: Hello, Jack.

R.C.: I didn't see you on the train.

R.B.: I was at the other end today.

R.C.: Thought it wouldn't be like you to miss it.

R.B.: Mm. Never have up to now, Jack.

R.C.: No. Cold this evening, isn't it?

R.B.: It is. It *is* cold.

(*They remove their overcoats and put them on the ground beside them.*)

R.C.: How long have we got to wait for the connection?

R.B.: Ten minutes, if it's on time. Try and get into the carriage near the engine – in the warm. What sort of day did the Stock Market have?

(*They are taking off their jackets.*)

R.C.: We were pretty lively today – everything's coming down, you know.

(*R.C. drops his trousers and steps out of them.*)

R.B.: Well, it's inevitable, isn't it?

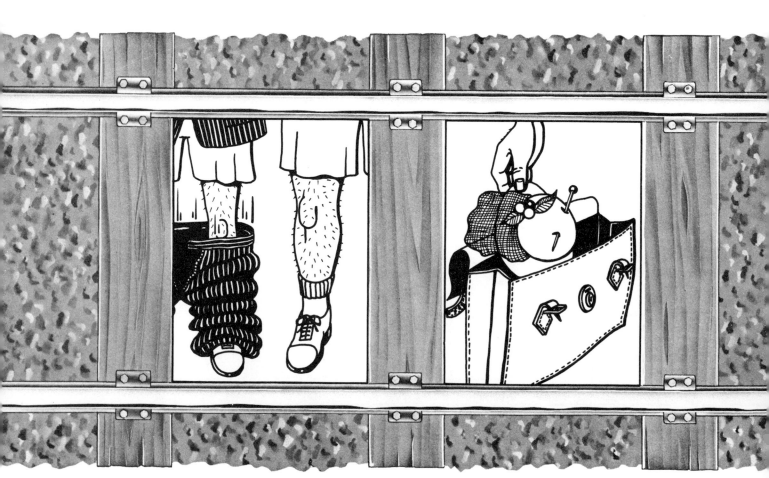

(*R.B. also removes his trousers.*)

R.C.: People haven't got the money to play with, (*unbuttoning his shirt*) not with the tax system in this country. (*Removes his shirt.*) They'd have the shirt off your back if they could.

R.B.: It's criminal. (*Removing his shirt.*) I've certainly got nothing to spare these days. It's hard enough trying to make ends meet. And the wife's no help either. (*Delving into his bag.*) Always spending money on some ridiculous item of clothing. (*He brings out of the bag a lady's hat with a veil and puts it on.*)

R.C.: That's just like a woman, isn't it? (*He takes out a mini-skirt from his bag, and puts it on.*) It's my daughter that's ruining me. Never out of the boutiques, spending a fortune. Takes absolutely no notice of me. (*Taking out a ladies' sweater and putting it on.*) Does

exactly as she thinks fit. No one would believe that I was the man of the house. (*Taking off his socks.*)

R.B.: (*During this has pulled up his light coloured socks, so that they become girls' knee-length ones.*) It's the modern generation, Jack. (*Takes frilly mini-dress out of his bag.*) You can't tell them anything. They just do things for kicks, nowadays. (*He steps into the dress and pulls it on.*)

R.C.: We never know where she is at night. (*He rolls his socks into balls.*) Worries me to death – there are some very odd people about you know, Ted. (*Tucks his socks under his sweater to make bosoms.*)

R.B.: (*Getting high heeled shoes out of his bag.*) Quite. Still I suppose we were considered odd when *we* were young. (*Putting on shoes.*)

R.C.: (*Also putting on high heeled shoes.*) Yes. We probably seem terribly dull and staid to them, just going about our business in the normal manner, travelling up on the train to work, day in, day out, always the same. I would say our lives must appear pretty colourless. (*He reaches into his bag and puts on a wildly colourful, jazzy hat.*)

R.B.: Well. I seem to be about ready. Are you? (*Takes handbag out of case.*)

R.C.: Yes, I'm ready. Bit of a nuisance all this, isn't it?

R.B.: Yes. Still, we live in hopes. Perhaps one day they'll build a *gentleman's* lavatory on this station.

(*They walk round a corner, and into a door marked "Ladies".*)

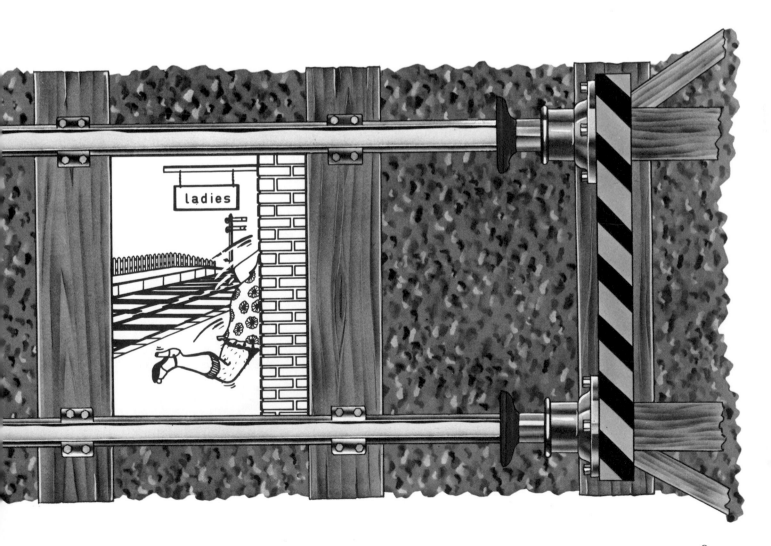

"I've Come Back"

A man sitting alone in a living room, staring into space. A woman enters, she wears a trench-coat, and when she speaks, speaks with a French accent. Film music over.

GIRL: Maurice. I have come back.

R.B.: (*Rising from his armchair.*) Madeleine!

(*They embrace each other, and background music is faded in.*)

GIRL: I did not mean to. I told myself I should not. And yet I could not bear it any longer – being away from this house – from all the little things that have become part of my life, in the three short months since I first met you. I said some very bitter things to you, I know, that night we quarrelled. Please forgive me. I *want* to look after you, to cook for you, to sew for you, to clean the house for you, to do the dishes for you. I want to! Oh please, please take me back! Please!

R.B.: But of course Madeleine! (*Calls out of door.*) Cynthia darling – the au pair girl's come back!

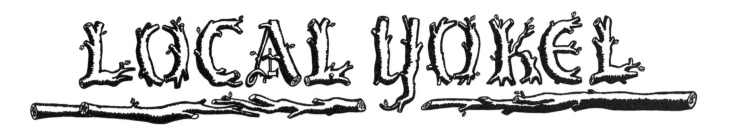

LOCAL YOKEL

An old yokel sits outside a pub, with his pint. A man in tweeds sees the yokel, and sits next to him. The yokel touches his hat.

MAN: Evening.

YOKEL: Evening, sir.

MAN: I'm trying to get to a place called Wareham, and I seem to have lost my way – I wonder if you could direct me?

YOKEL: Thankee, sir, that's very kind, I'll have a pint of mild. (*He downs his beer, and empties his glass in one.*)

MAN: Oh. Er – miss! (*To a fat young girl clearing glasses.*) Er – two pints of mild, please. (*She goes.*) It's been a nice day. Not a sign of rain.

YOKEL: The peas need the water, sir. Shrivelled up they are. Terrible.

MAN: Yes, I suppose they do. Have you lived all your life here?

YOKEL: Not yet, sir, no, no.

          (*A pause*)

MAN: Quiet round here, isn't it?

YOKEL: Ar – you wait till tonight.

MAN: Oh – livens up a bit, does it?

YOKEL: No – gets quieter. No comparison. Gets deathly quiet about these parts at night. People die of the quiet round here sometimes.

          (*The girl brings the beer.*)

MAN: Oh, I rather like the quiet. My fiancée is meeting me at Wareham – we decided to have a weekend in the country away from the noise. We're staying at the Boar's Head.

YOKEL: Very nice.

(*A pause*).

MAN: It looks like being a lovely night.

YOKEL: Certainly sounds like it. Cheers. (*He drinks.*)

MAN: Oh – cheers. No, I like to be quiet.

YOKEL: Well, there's some as do and there's some as don't. There's an old saying round these parts: "Stile and Hedge, Water's Edge, Mills a-turning, Corns a-burning, silence reigns upon the valley, John and Mary up the alley."

MAN: What does that mean?

YOKEL: I don't know, I'm a stranger round here.

MAN: Oh, you don't live in the village?

YOKEL: Oh yes, I live here, but the other folks treat me as a
              stranger.

MAN: Why?

YOKEL: I'm strange.

MAN: Ah. I see. Er – look, I must find my way to Wareham
              tonight – is it far?

YOKEL: Well, thankee sir – I'll have the same again. (*He drains
              his beer at one go again.*) Greta! Same again! (*A slight
              pause.*) You staying round these parts, sir?

MAN: No, just passing through.

YOKEL: Oh, that's a pity. You'll miss the Willy racing. That's
              tomorrow.

MAN: The Willy racing? What's that?

YOKEL: Ain't you never heard of the Willy racing? Ooh, that's
              the best day of the year round here. Everybody gets up
              early, and we all have breakfast on the Green, all
              together – rum, black treacle, and sausages and a cup of
              tea. Then all the girls under thirty rush off into the woods
              woods to pick puss-willows, and all the men over sixty
              rush after them. That's a wonderful race to watch, that
              is. You didn't ought to miss that.

MAN: Why is it called "Willy racing"?

YOKEL: Well, when an old man runs after a girl, into the woods,
              it's a question of will he or won't he you see, sir. I came
              second last year.

MAN: Did you?

YOKEL: No sir, that's why I only came second.

MAN: Oh, I see. (*The beer arrives.*)

YOKEL: Good health, sir.

MAN: Cheers. (*To barmaid.*) Would you take these glasses?
         (*The girl collects them up.*) Er – Do you know the way to
         Wareham?

YOKEL: She don't know – she ain't never worn 'em, have you
         Greta? (*She giggles and goes off.*) None of the women wear
         'em round here. They don't believe in 'em.

MAN: What?

YOKEL: Glasses.

MAN: What glasses?

YOKEL: I thought you mentioned glasses.

MAN: I did. But I was talking about . . . Oh, never mind.

YOKEL: Ah. Oh well, I must be off. (*Rises.*) "To bed betimes,
         and up anon, the thistle has the bristles on." Good
         night, sir.

MAN: How am I going to get to Wareham?

YOKEL: No thankee kindly, sir, I've drunk enough tonight.

MAN: Aren't you going to buy *me* a drink?

YOKEL: Eh?

MAN: I've bought you three drinks. Isn't it time you bought
         me one?

YOKEL: Oh, sorry sir. I do beg your pardon. What must you
         think of me? It's straight up the road about three miles.
         You can't miss it. Good night! (*He exits.*)

REACHING AGREEMENT

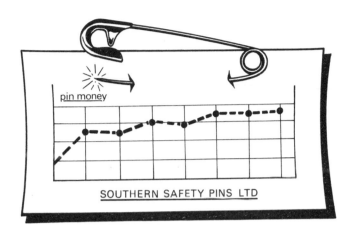

*(Four old men at a board meeting. They all look alike. One –
Mr. Green – is asleep.)*

R.B.: Now gentlemen, we have called this meeting
because the shareholders are worried the
company is not paying enough attention to
improving and modernising the production
lines. Southern Safety Pins Ltd. is a well-
established firm, and sales are steady. However,
there is room for improvement and we have to
discuss ways of increasing the shareholders
dividends – not to put too fine a point on it.

R.C.: But surely, Hopkins, if we don't put too fine a
point on it, the safety pin won't do up. And
that's your export trade up the spout. That
would be fatal.

JONES: How about making the spout more rounded?
I'm sure that by and large, people prefer a
rounded spout.

R.B.: Well, large people would, certainly. I should
have thought it was a question of individual
taste.

R.C.: I disagree. It doesn't matter what things taste like, as long as it says "Delicious, mouth-watering and fresh" on the packet. Mark my words.

JONES: That's not a bad idea. Mark the words in red on every tin. They'll sell like hot cakes.

R.C.: Perhaps we could install ovens in the supermarkets to keep the cakes hot. That would put us streets ahead of our competitors.

R.B.: Well, I suppose street-trading is certainly something to be considered. Although our conditions of licence would probably put the tin hat on that.

R.C.: Hardly likely to increase trade, I would have thought. I mean if I saw a man standing by an oven in the street with a tin hat on, I'd think it was a little queer.

R.B.: Well, they could wear notices saying "I am not a little queer." And they could push things through letter boxes, which would appeal to the housewife.

R.C.: Yes, letter boxes are certainly worth looking into. Perhaps as an experiment, we could try it out in certain key places.

JONES: Well, the best key place I know is under the mat, by the back door.

R.B.:   True. You know, these keys could open up all sorts of possibilities with the house-owners.

R.C.:   And if we *did* get the owners to open up their houses, the public could be admitted at a nominal fee – and we'd beat our competitors on their own ground.

R.B.:   I think it will work – and not only on our own ground, but when we are playing away as well. Of course, we need someone to really get the team up to scratch. The question is, who's best?

R.C.:   He used to be a famous footballer. Georgie Best.

R.B.:   Then he's the very man! Appoint him to the board, and get the public to open their houses.

R.C.:   Do you think we can do this? Get the public's houses open?

R.B.:   What's the time?

R.C.: Ten to twelve.

R.B.: Is it? Oh yes, they must be open by now. Come on, I'll buy you one.

(*They all get up and wake up Mr. Green.*)

R.B.: Come on, Green, the pubs are open.

R.C.: We're going to vote Georgie Best on to the Board. (*Mr. Green gets up.*)

JONES: Well, that's that then.

R.C.: Yes – nice to feel you've got something done, isn't it?

R.B.: Quite. All you have to do is get round a table and talk about it.

(*They go out to the pub.*)